a gift to:

my Special Friend
Joanne

from: Clare

I pray at this time,
some quotes may
put a smile on
Your face.
Love You!

snapshots of heaven

JOYCE VOLLMER BROWN

illustrated by

GWENDOLYN BABBITT

GIFT BOOKS

BOK 3034

COUNTRYMAN

This edition published in 2001 by J. Countryman, a division
of Thomas Nelson, Inc., exclusively for Hallmark Cards, Inc.

Project Editor: Terri Gibbs

All Scripture quotations in this book are from the New
International Version of the Bible (NIV), copyright ©1983
by the International Bible Society and are used
by permission of Zondervan Bible Publishers.

Designed by Left Coast Design Inc. Portland, Oregon.

ISBN: 08499-9575-2 (Hallmark edition)

Printed in China

www.hallmark.com

To David, Ryan, and Phil:
May the circle be unbroken
on that glorious shore.

In Heaven . . .

In heaven...

We'll arm wrestle with Samson, go fishing with
Peter, ask Noah how he got all the animals
into the ark, hear what Daniel was thinking
as he looked at those lions, and listen to
Mary's stories about Jesus' childhood.

In heaven...

We'll swap jokes with Chuck Swindoll, sing songs with Steve Green, play catch with Orel Hershiser, and take hikes with Joni Eareckson Tada.

In heaven...

We'll be reunited with dear friends and
family members who have died.

We'll get to know countless generations of our
ancestors.

We'll meet people whose lives we touched in
ways we never knew.

And we'll never run out of things to talk about.

In heaven...

We'll be surrounded by heroes—the finest,
brightest, bravest, most noble people from
all over the world throughout all of time.
And we'll never run out of things to talk about.

In heaven...

We'll get to know angels who were on hand
when the earth was created, angels who sang
to the shepherds that first Christmas, and
angels who watched over us on earth.

In heaven...

Angels will tell us how they learned from us!
(Ephesians 3:10)

In heaven...

> There will only be hellos—no good-byes.
>
> There won't be any broken hearts or broken homes.
>
> Love will never die.

In heaven...

Our hearts will always be wide open;
we'll have nothing to hide because all of our
guilt will be gone.

In heaven...

We'll share
everything
we have
because
we'll never
worry about
not having
enough.

In heaven...

No one will ever be angry, rude, or unkind.
Everyone will always be incredibly nice.

In heaven...

No one will have a big ego. Everyone will be
poor in spirit—amazed by the grace that
brought them there.

In heaven...

Instead of competing against one
another, we'll cheer for each
other.
We'll never feel awkward or
dumb because no one will ever
look down on us.

In heaven...

We will still be individuals with
unique appearances, talents,
and personalities.
We'll not only be ourselves, but all
that God meant us to be.

In heaven...

We'll be different
without having
differences.
There won't
be any
Democrats
or Republicans,
conservatives
or liberals, Baptists or Lutherans.
No prejudice or discrimination, arguments or
disagreements.

There will be perfect harmony because
everyone will have one mind (the mind
of Christ) and one goal (to glorify God).

In heaven...

> There won't be any strangers.
> Everyone will be part of one HUGE, loving
>   family.

In heaven...

> We'll love those we loved on earth a thousand
> times more, and we'll love thousands of others
> as well.

In heaven...

> We'll accept each other totally—just as we
> are—because we'll all be perfect.
> No one will have any faults or flaws!

In heaven...

> We'll be surrounded by people with unlimited
> capacity to love.

In heaven...

> There won't be any locked doors or security
> alarms.

In heaven...

> There will be no need for cameras or
> scrapbooks.
> We won't need to capture wonderful moments
> and sights because every day will be a
> magnificent memory in the making, and
> beyond each turn will be a scene more
> breathtaking than the last.

In heaven...

There won't be
any bills in the
mailbox.
There won't
be any
commercials,
salespeople,
or phone
solicitors
because
everything
will be free!

In heaven...

> Instead of the government taking more and
> more and more,
> the government will give and give and give.

In heaven...

> There won't be any sleazy campaigns or
> corrupt politicians.
> The government will be flawless—with officials
> appointed by God.

In heaven...

Retarded children will have mental abilities
greater than earthly geniuses.
The blind will see, the deaf will sing, the
crippled will dance, and the poor will wear
fine clothes and live in luxury.

In heaven...

People who were "nobodies" on earth
will be put in charge of whole cities.

In heaven...

> God will give bigger rewards to Christians with
>   great attitudes than those with great
>   achievements.
> He'll reward the faithful more than the
>   successful.

In heaven...

We'll be treated royally wherever we go.
We'll never be put on hold or have to wait
in long lines.
We'll be
    known by
    name—
    not an I.D.
    number.

In heaven...

We'll believe everything we hear.
There won't be any slanted news,
distorted facts, or exaggerated stories.
No deceptions or lies. Truth will reign.

In heaven...

The news will always be something to
celebrate.
There won't be a single sad or disturbing
story.

In heaven...

We'll never have to do anything we don't want
to, and we'll never run out of things we
want to do!

In heaven...

We'll not only be adopted into God's family,
but into His business as well.
It will be such a privilege to have a hand
in something so big and so important.

In heaven...

Everyone will have work they love to do.
Work will never be boring, stressful, unfulfilling,
or unappreciated.

Success will be
guaranteed
because
we'll never
fail or
make
mistakes.

In heaven...

Many people will
have to find
new vocations.
There won't be
a need for
doctors,
nurses,
pharmacists,
dentists, lawyers, social workers,
beauticians, psychiatrists, insurance agents,
soldiers, bankers, undertakers, tax collectors,
police, or repairmen.

In heaven...

We'll be like
children in
all the good
ways:
innocent,
carefree,
open, and
fun-loving.
We'll trust
everyone,
be eager to learn,
and be filled with wonder.

In heaven...

We will no longer need faith to believe
because we'll see and know.

In heaven...

> We won't pray any more.
>
> We'll talk to God face to face.
>
> We won't have any sins to confess or needs to ask for.
>
> We will praise and thank God without ceasing.

In heaven...

There won't be any churches or temples.
Every inch of heaven will be holy and pure
and filled with God's presence.

In heaven...

Wherever we go, we'll be home. We'll never wish we were somewhere else, doing something else, or with someone else.

In heaven...

There will be only two kinds of tears—
tears of laughter and tears of joy.
We will never be
    angry,
      lonely,
        frustrated,
          frightened,
            discouraged,
              overwhelmed,
                dissatisfied,
                  or depressed.

In heaven...

We'll have such a fantastic time that
decades, even centuries will fly by.

In heaven...

It won't be hard to be good. The Tempter
won't be around to trip us up.

In heaven...

We won't need cars, trains, or planes.

We'll move throughout the galaxy in an instant.

If something gets in our way, we'll just go
   through it!

In heaven...

We'll know life without
bounds—with
no restrictions
from budgets,
health, or physical
abilities.
No speed limits, time
limits, or red tape.
No limits to love, patience, or understanding.
We'll be free from fear, doubt, and sin—
free to be all we were created to be.

In heaven...

Nothing will seem impossible.
Nothing will ever go wrong because God's will,
will always be done.

In heaven...

We won't say, "How are you?" in greeting
because the answer will always be the
same:
"Fantastic!" or "Incredible!" or
"Unbelievable!"

In heaven...

No one will warn us to "Be careful" because
there won't be any dangers.

In heaven...

> We won't say, "I wish . . ." because every longing we've ever had will be satisfied. We'll be totally content.

In heaven...

> We won't say, "If only . . ." because we won't have any regrets.

In heaven...

> We won't say, "What if . . .". There will be nothing to worry about because we won't be able to lose any blessings.

In heaven...

> We'll never describe anything by saying,
> "It was good while it lasted" because
> everything good will last forever.

In heaven...

If we ask someone, "What's new?" we'll sit
    and listen for hours—maybe even days.
There will always be countless new delights
    and discoveries to share.

In heaven...

We won't use the word "too."

The weather will never be too hot or too cold.

No distance will be too great. No place will be too crowded.

We'll never have too much on our mind or too many things to do. Everything will always be just right.

In heaven...

We'll say "Hallelujah!" "Hosanna!" "Praise God!"
and "Thank You, Jesus!" over and over.

In heaven...

We won't spoil things like we did on earth.

The air will stay fresh and clean.

Rivers will sparkle.

No garbage will mar the beauty of the

landscape.

In heaven...

Memories of earth's greatest glories will
seem drab and paltry.

Diamond-capped waves,
   crimson sunsets,
   star-studded skies,
   ice-crystal
   covered trees
   sparkling in the sun—
   will be faint shadows
   of the breathtaking
   beauty surrounding us.

In heaven...

We'll live in
a new
land
where
everything
will be
bigger,
brighter, and better
than anything we've ever imagined.

It will be 1,500 miles long, 1,500 miles wide, and
1,500 miles high (big enough so millions of
people will have plenty of room).

In heaven...

The city's walls will be covered with jewels
of many colors and have gates cut into
giant pearls. (We'll be able to leave the
city through these gates and travel
throughout the universe.)

Its shining streets will be made of transparent
gold.

God's throne will be in the center of the city.
Behind the throne a beautiful rainbow will
remind us of His loving grace.

In heaven...

Even though there won't be a sun or moon, we won't need any candles or lights because the whole place will be filled with warm, glowing light—from the glory of God.

The heavenly city will be a city of life.

The river of the water of life, clear as crystal,
   will flow from the throne down the main street
   of the city.

Trees of life will grow on either side of it. Each
   tree will be like a fruit-of-the-month club,
   bearing a different kind of crop each month.

The curse and all of its negative effects will
   be removed.

There will be lush, gorgeous vegetation (like the
   Garden of Eden).

Fruit won't decay. Flowers won't wither. Trees and
   plants will flourish—undamaged by insects,
   unstunted by disease, uncrowded by weeds.

In heaven...

> We'll each have a wonderful home
> custom built to suit us, lavishly
> decorated to reflect our tastes,
> lovingly prepared with everything
> we need to be happy and
> comfortable.

In heaven...

Nothing will break, fade,
wear out, or decay.
Everything will always be
fresh and new.

In heaven...
Nothing will
ever smell bad.

In heaven...

Even the animals will live peacefully.

Wolves and lambs, calves and lions,

bears and snakes will live side by side.

In heaven...

Everything will be pure and unadulterated.

All of our thoughts will be holy.

Our love will be completely unselfish,

our motives unmixed,

our behavior faultless,

our worship perfect,

and our joy absolute.

In heaven...

It will always be spring,
   always be morning,
   always the beginning
   —never the end.

In heaven...

Every day will be new and different.

There will be never-ending variety.

Our wonder will never wear off.

In heaven...

One day will be better than a thousand
on earth, and we'll have thousands of
thousands of days times thousands of
thousands of thousands . . .

In heaven...

Storehouses of blessings are ready and
waiting for us.

In heaven...

As God's
   adopted
   children
   we'll
   receive
   an
   inheritance
of untold wealth, countless
rewards for every tiny act of obedience
and service we ever performed, and an
endless shower of gifts to demonstrate His
never-ending love.

In heaven...

We'll finally understand how wide and long
and high and deep God's love for us is.

In heaven...

We'll never be anxious or impatient for the
future because our attention will be
totally captivated by unimaginable joy
and miraculous wonders of the present.

In heaven...

Every day will be like our birthday, Valentine's
Day, and Christmas
combined.

Life will be so exciting
that we'll feel like
kids who don't want
to go to bed
because they're
afraid of missing
something.

And we'll never have
to, since we won't
need to sleep.

In heaven...

 There won't be any cosmetic counters;
  every woman will be gorgeous naturally.

In heaven...

 There won't be any wrinkled faces, gray
  hair, or bald heads; no false teeth or
  bifocals, no stooped shoulders, arthritic
  joints, or fading memories.
 Everyone will be in the prime of life forever.

In heaven...

> We'll experience wonders no eyes have ever
>   seen, no ears have ever heard, no hearts
>   have even hoped for.
> Senses we have now will be heightened, and
>   we'll have new senses as well.

In heaven...

> We'll probably know one another
> instantly just as
> Peter, James,
> and John
> knew Moses
> and Elijah
> on the mountaintop.

In heaven...

We'll have unimaginable abilities.

We may be telepathic and read each other's
minds. (That will be OK since we won't have
any unkind or impure thoughts.)

In heaven...

> We won't wish we could change a single thing
> about ourselves!
> Our bodies, personalities, characters, thoughts,
> and actions will all be perfect.

In heaven...

> We will talk and
> act and think
> and love—like
> Christ.

In heaven...

We'll never stop
    learning and
    growing. We'll
    develop our
    gifts and
    abilities
    and
    discover
    talents we never knew we had.
We'll accomplish things we dreamed of,
    but didn't have the time or opportunity
    to do on earth.

In heaven...

Like a blushing bride whose eyes focus
on her beloved rather than her own
beauty, we will hardly notice our own
glory.

All eyes will be fixed upon God. Every look will
be filled with love, every heart will be
filled with wonder.

In heaven...

We'll be crowned with majesty and honor. Like kings and queens, we'll rule the earth with Christ and judge angels. Yet we'll cast our crowns at Jesus' feet without hesitating.

In heaven...

Although our lives will be filled with
unlimited blessings, none will compare
with the joy of walking and talking with
Jesus and knowing God intimately—the
way He has always known us.
There won't be any veil between us or any
door we must knock on.
We won't have to wait for Him to agree
to receive us.
He will always welcome us, always be
delighted to spend time with us.

In heaven...

We'll feel more at home than we ever did
on earth because we'll be with our
Father.

We'll see how tenderly He loves us each
time we look in His eyes.

Our hearts will thrill as He tells us how
proud He is of us.

He'll protect us from harm and keep all evil
from us.

He'll patiently teach us, answer our
questions, and gently mold our spirit
and character to make us more like
Him.

©Gwendolyn Babbitt

In heaven...

We'll lose ourselves and our self-centered
focus.

Our thoughts will be consumed with God's
awesome glory, power, and love.

In heaven...

We'll worship

effortlessly without
distractions,

openly without
self-consciousness,

confidently with no insecurity about
where we stand,

completely with no guilt holding us back,

spontaneously and continuously with
an overflowing heart.

In heaven...

We will love God
the way He
deserves to
be loved.
After ten
thousand
years pass
we'll still
be falling
deeper
and deeper
in love with Him.

In heaven...

A never-ending "welcome home" party is
waiting for our arrival.

Our heavenly Father will come to greet us
with open, loving arms.

Jesus, our older brother, will bring us a robe
and a crown.

And our hearts will be overcome with joy and
relief to finally be home to stay.

Afterword

The good news is that God will welcome all
into heaven who have welcomed Him into
their hearts.